5/11 ox

10/10

WITHDRAWN

R

Pebble® Plus

Asian Animals
Rhinoceroses

by Joanne Mattern

Consulting Editor: Gail Saunders-Smith, PhD

Content Consultant: Tanya Dewey, PhD
University of Michigan Museum of Zoology

CAPSTONE PRESS
a capstone imprint

Pebble Plus is published by Capstone Press,
151 Good Counsel Drive, P.O. Box 669, Mankato, Minnesota 56002.
www.capstonepress.com

092009
005618CGS10

 Books published by Capstone Press are manufactured with paper
containing at least 10 percent post-consumer waste.

Library of Congress Cataloging-in-Publication Data
Mattern, Joanne, 1963–
    Rhinoceroses / by Joanne Mattern.
    p. cm. — (Pebble plus. Asian animals)
    Includes bibliographical references and index.
    Summary: "Simple text and photographs present rhinoceroses, how they look, where they live, and what
they do" — Provided by publisher.
    ISBN 978-1-4296-4031-2 (library binding)
    ISBN 978-1-4296-4846-2 (paperback)
    1. Rhinoceroses — Juvenile literature. I. Title. II. Series.
QL737.U63M386 2010
599.66'8 — dc22
           2009028644

Editorial Credits

Katy Kudela, editor; Matt Bruning, designer; Svetlana Zhurkin, media researcher; Eric Manske. production specialist

Photo Credits

Alamy/Dinodia Images, 21; Corbis/Charles Philip Cangialosi, 5; Corbis/Frank Lane Picture Agency/Terry Whittaker, 17;
Nature Picture Library/Anup Shah, 9; Peter Arnold/Biosphoto/Alain Compost, 7, 13; Peter Arnold/Biosphoto/
Tony Crocetta, 19; Peter Arnold/C. Huetter, cover; Photolibrary/Andoni Canela, 11; Photolibrary/Oxford Scientific/
Mary Plage, 15; Shutterstock/Dmitry Pichugin, 1

Note to Parents and Teachers

The Asian Animals series supports national science standards related to life science.
This book describes and illustrates rhinoceroses. The images support early readers in
understanding the text. The repetition of words and phrases helps early readers learn new
words. This book also introduces early readers to subject-specific vocabulary words, which are
defined in the Glossary section. Early readers may need assistance to read some words and to
use the Table of Contents, Glossary, Read More, Internet Sites, and Index sections of the book.

Table of Contents

Living in Asia

Asia is home to three kinds
of rhinoceroses.
They are the Indian,
Javan, and Sumatran.

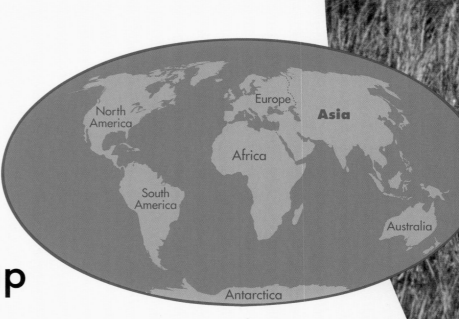

World Map

Indian rhino

Rhinos graze in southeastern
Asia's swamps and forests.
These animals live alone
most of the time.

where rhinoceroses live

Javan rhino

Up Close!

Rhinos are heavy.

Strong legs and large feet

carry their weight.

They may look slow.

But rhinos can run fast.

Indian rhino

Rhinos have thick, gray skin.

They roll in mud to cool off.

The mud protects their skin

from sunburn and bug bites.

Sumatran rhino

On their noses, rhinos have
horns made of keratin.
They look ready to fight.
But Asian rhinos fight with
their teeth, not their horns.

Sumatran rhino

13

Eating and Drinking

Rhinos eat leaves and grass.

They drink water

from ponds and streams.

Javan rhino

15

Rhinos have strong lips

to pull food into their mouths.

Their sharp teeth

grind leaves and grass.

Sumatran rhino

Staying Safe

A mother rhino

always protects her calf.

She keeps her baby safe

from predators.

Indian rhino with young

19

Rhinos are endangered.

Poachers kill rhinos

for their horns.

But other people are making

safe places for rhinos to live.

Indian rhino

21

Glossary

calf — a young rhinoceros

endangered — in danger of dying out

graze — to eat grass and other plants growing on the ground

grind — to crush something into a powder

keratin — a hard material that makes up a rhino's horn; keratin is also found in human fingernails and hair.

poacher — a person who hunts protected animals

predator — an animal that hunts other animals for food

protect — to keep safe

swamp — an area of wet, spongy ground with lots of plants

Read More

Kalman, Bobbie. *Endangered Rhinoceros.* Earth's Endangered Animals. New York: Crabtree Publishing, 2004.

Latta, Jan. *Rudy the Rhinoceros.* Wild Animal Families. Milwaukee: Gareth Stevens Publishing, 2007.

Suen, Anastasia. *A Rhinoceros Grows Up.* Wild Animals. Minneapolis: Picture Window Books, 2006.

Internet Sites

FactHound offers a safe, fun way to find Internet sites related to this book. All of the sites on FactHound have been researched by our staff.

Here's all you do:

Visit *www.facthound.com*

FactHound will fetch the best sites for you!

Index

Word Count: 160
Grade: 1
Early-Intervention Level: 18